Meet US Under the Night SKy

Written by Andrew F. Johnson   Illustrated by Jennifer Johnson Haywood

Kids can become official Junior Rangers! There are hundreds of different Junior Ranger programs available throughout the United States. Ask at any National Park Service (NPS), state park, or other public land visitor center to see if a local program is offered.

Complete the fun activities, games and puzzles in the Junior Ranger packet. Then you may stop by a visitor center to receive your Junior Ranger certificate, badge, patch, or pin.

For Space Camp alumni Drew and Aidan

As our population grows, there are more lights making the Night Sky harder to see.
This is called light pollution. To best see the Night Sky, find a location with few or no lights.
Some cities and parks are working to reduce this problem.

Published by HAYWOOD STUDIOS INC.
Hastings, Michigan 49058 U.S.A.
Jr. RangerLand™ is a registered trademark of Haywood Studios Inc.

Printed in the United States of America

Second Printing, First Edition 2017

Publisher's Cataloging-in-Publication data

Names: Johnson, Andrew F., author | Haywood, Jennifer Johnson, illustrator.
Title: Meet us under the night sky / written by Andrew F. Johnson ; illustrated by Jennifer Johnson Haywood.
Description: Hastings, MI: Haywood Studios, Inc., 2017.
Identifiers: ISBN 978-0-9888128-2-6 | LCCN 2017941399
Subjects: LCSH Outer space--Juvenile poetry. | Outer space--Poetry. | Astronomy--Juvenile literature. | Solar system--Juvenile literature. | BISAC JUVENILE NONFICTION / Science & Nature / Astronomy
Classification: LCC QB46 .J64 | DDC 520--dc23

For more information about Jr. RangerLand products please visit our website: www.jr-rangerland.com

Other books in this series include:

Meet Us at the National Parks

Meet Us on the Trail

Andrew F. Johnson is a retired businessman who enjoys golf, photography, creative writing, woodworking, and bridge, among other interests. He likes traveling with his wife, Pat. He resides in Hastings, Michigan. He and his wife have two children and five grandchildren living in the area.

Jennifer Johnson Haywood is the president and co-owner of Jr. RangerLand. She has a degree in illustration from Kendall College of Art and Design and a master's degree in illustration from Syracuse University. She lives in Hastings, Michigan with her husband and three children. Together, they spend much of their time visiting U.S. National Parks, state parks, and other historic and recreational sites.

The cosmos holds a zillion things,
from twinkling stars to planet rings.
I'm Ranger Land. Let's go walk.
It's time to have a Night Sky talk.

The age of space is just a guess:
12 billion years, more or less.

Stars and novae create light. Watch them sparkle in the night.

Stars shine, astronomers know; burning gases make them glow.

Millions of stars form each day,
and millions more fade away.

Nebulae are dust and gas but they look like colored glass.

There's a Horsehead, Eagle and Ring. One makes a butterfly's wing.

Our galaxy is the Milky Way with billions of stars on display.

When many stars make formations they are known as constellations. Look in space. Select a spot.

Connect the stars like "dot to dot." Behold a dragon. Find a harp. Discover fish that look like carp.

The Big Dipper's fun to find
with seven stars all aligned.

Polaris

Big
Dipper

To find Polaris use this guide: Draw a line from the Dipper's side.

That's not one star. See the luster. Many stars make a cluster.

A meteor's tail never stays.

A comet's tail lasts for days.

When the sun creates a flare,

the Northern Lights dance on air.

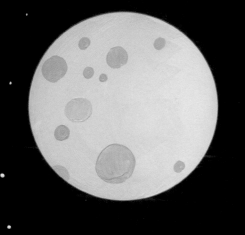

Planets and moons, it is known, make no light of their own,
but our sun, a ball of fire, makes the light that we require.

19

Planets from Earth, that you can see, are Venus, Mars, and Mercury.

You'll spot Saturn, that's for sure, followed next by Jupiter.

Use a scope and you can view Uranus and Neptune too.

21

The earth spins daily like a top.
Around it goes and doesn't stop.

Some planets have moons. Some have none. Planet Earth has only one.

It's plain to see, off in space,
our moon has craters on its face.

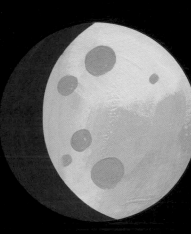

Waxing Gibbous

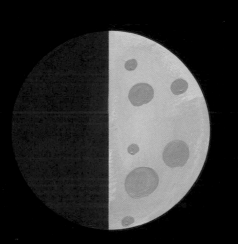

First Quarter Moon

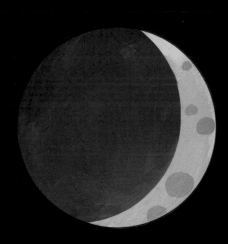

Waxing Crescent

New Moon

A moon that's new won't show at all.

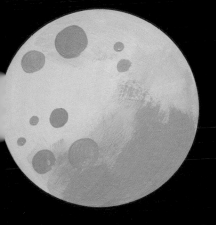

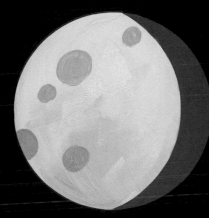

Full Moon

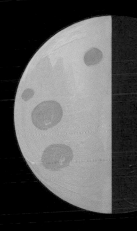

Waning Gibbous

Last Quarter Moon

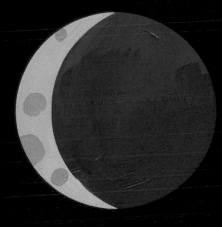

Waning Crescent

A moon that's full looks like a ball.

Sun and Moon with Earth between: An eclipse is seldom seen.

28

Darkness falls. The sky is clear.
Watch for stars as they appear.
Use a scope or just your eye.
Enjoy the beauty of the sky.

Meet Us Under the Night Sky – Additional information and corresponding page numbers

1. The cosmos is made of everything in space. It contains galaxies, stars, solar systems, planets, moons, asteroids, comets, novae, quasars, pulsars, dark matter, black holes, solar wind, and much more.

2-3. The current estimated age of the Universe is about 12-14 billion years.

4-5. Some objects that create light are stars, galaxies, novae, nebulae, quasars, and pulsars. Stars are huge balls of burning gases. They create heat and light. It is estimated 5,000-10,000 new stars form in the time it takes to blink your eye. Also, that number die.

6-7. Nebulae can be dying stars, but also a nursery for new stars.

8-9. A galaxy is a group of billions of stars and all nearby planets, comets, asteroids, etc. There are an estimated 100 billion galaxies.

10-11. Constellations are named star formations and also include nearby objects. People dreamed up some of these patterns many years ago. There are 88 official constellations of all sizes and shapes that make a complete atlas of the sky. Thirty constellations can be seen from the northern hemisphere, although only five can be seen all year.

12-13. The Big Dipper is an asterism, not a constellation. It is in the constellation Ursa Major, the big bear. It's not a straight line of stars, but a grouping that takes the shape of a ladle, or "dipper," when connected. Polaris or the North Star, is always visible from the northern hemisphere. It is used for navigation.

14. A globular cluster is hundreds or thousands of stars held together by gravity. A cluster is many galaxies held together by gravity.

15. Meteoroids are rocks in space. When they enter Earth's atmosphere, they become a meteor and burn up, creating a momentary streak of light. Comets are large collections of rock, dust, ice, and gases. They orbit the sun. As they come close to the sun, they warm and the materials vaporize causing a very long tail. A comet's tail may be seen for days or even weeks.

16-17. Solar flares are eruptions on the sun, which in turn, create the Northern Lights on Earth.

18-19. Our sun is a star. It is as big as one million Earths. It looks small because it is far away. Planets, moons, comets, asteroids, and more reflect a star's light, like being lit by a flashlight.

20-21. Our sun has at least eight planets in its solar system. From the sun, they are Mercury, Venus, Earth, Mars, Jupiter, Saturn, Uranus, and Neptune. Earth is sometimes called the Blue Planet, because of its oceans and other bodies of water. Pluto was once called a planet, but because it is so small, is no longer considered one. There may be a recently discovered new planet called Planet 9, but little is known about it yet. Mercury, Venus, Earth, and Mars are rocky planets. Saturn, Jupiter, Uranus, and Neptune are balls of gases. The gaseous planets have rings. The rings of Saturn are the brightest.

22-23. The Earth rotates once per day and orbits the sun once per year.

24. Our eight planets have a total of 173 moons: Mercury and Venus have none. Earth has one. Mars has two; Jupiter, 67; Saturn, 62; Uranus, 27; and Neptune, 14. More may be discovered.

25. Asteroids crashing on the moon caused the craters we see.

26-27. Our moon circles Earth every 27 days. It goes from new to full and back again in that time.

28. A lunar eclipse happens when all three bodies are aligned and the Earth blocks the sun's light, casting a shadow on the moon. Usually the moon glows, reflecting the light from the sun. A solar eclipse occurs when the moon passes between Earth and the sun.

29. The Universe and our knowledge of it are constantly changing. Stars collide. Galaxies collide. Black Holes are formed. Asteroids smash into planets. Stars die. And the technology we use to study the Universe is constantly improving. Our ideas change too. Pluto was a planet. Then it was demoted to a dwarf planet. Planet 9 is 20 times farther from the Sun than Neptune. We don't know if it is rocky or gaseous or if it has moons or even if it really is a planet. Change is the only constant.